CLASSIC DIESEL YE
CUMBRIAN COAS

PAUL SHANNON

No. 40063 passes Drigg with the 17.14 Workington-Dover Speedlink train on 12 July 1983. The front portion comprises one bogie tank and five two-axle tanks, all carrying sodium tripolyphosphate from Corkickle to West Thurrock.

1

© Paul Shannon, 2023
First published in the United Kingdom, 2023,
by Stenlake Publishing Ltd.
www.stenlake.co.uk
ISBN 978-1-84033-966-6

The publishers regret that they cannot supply
copies of any pictures featured in this book.

Printed by
P2D Books, 1 Newlands Rd, Westoning, Bedford MK45 5LD

No. 60060 *James Watt* crosses the Esk Estuary with the 11.55 Maryport-Carnforth coal train on 27 February 1993. This was a short-term contract to move Cumbrian coal to Padiham Power Station and was the last rail traffic to be loaded at Maryport.

Introduction

The 120-mile route from Carlisle to Carnforth around the Cumbrian Coast was a fascinating corner of the British railway network in the 1980s and early 1990s, with a good number of freight flows producing a variety of diesel traction and rolling-stock and a signalling system that was still largely based on Victorian principles. While passenger services north of Barrow-in-Furness were dominated by Class 108 DMUs, those between Barrow-in-Furness and Carnforth were often locomotive-hauled. Also worthy of mention is the Whitehaven postal train, which survived until 1991.

Historically, the Cumbrian Coast Line was the product of several different railway companies, whose tracks were gradually linked to provide a coherent through route. The first stretch to open was the Maryport & Carlisle Railway in 1845, while further south the Furness Railway completed two short lines radiating from Barrow-in-Furness in 1846, extending northwards to Foxfield and Broughton-in-Furness in 1848. The Whitehaven Junction Railway and the Whitehaven & Furness Junction Railway between them plugged the gap between Whitehaven and the Furness Railway at Foxfield in stages between 1848 and 1852. The Furness Railway reached eastwards to Ulverston in 1854, and the Ulverston & Lancaster Railway completed the final link to Carnforth in 1857.

Just over a century later, the infamous 1963 report *The Reshaping of British Railways* proposed the closure of the central part of the Cumbrian Coast Line, which would have left just Carlisle to Whitehaven and Barrow-in-Furness to Carnforth as separate branch lines. In the event, while the various railways heading inland from the coast all closed, the coastal route survived. However, the line was a low priority for investment. Changes to the infrastructure were mainly minor, such as the

Class 108 cars M54243 and M53959 call at Millom with the 12.08 from Lancaster to Whitehaven on 12 July 1983.

resignalling of Dalston in 1973 as part of the West Coast Main Line scheme and the closure of Nethertown loop in 1977.

By the early 1980s, all the small station goods yards on the Cumbrian Coast had closed, but the line still carried a healthy mixture of freight. At the northern end of the line, there were regular flows of oil to Dalston, chemicals to Wigton, coal from Maryport, various traffics to and from Workington Docks, steel products to and from Workington Steelworks, coal from Whitehaven and chemicals to and from Corkickle. The nuclear reprocessing plant at Sellafield produced regular flask trains from power stations around the country as well as inward deliveries of chemicals. At the south end of the line, Barrow Docks generated some residual coal and scrap metal traffic as well as occasional imports of nuclear flasks. Ulverston Goods Yard handled occasional trainloads of oil, while the Glaxo works on the east side of Ulverston received chemicals by rail.

The earliest images in this album show Classes 25 and 40 still active on a variety of freight workings. There were also the ubiquitous Class 47s, which worked some of the freight as well as most of the loco-hauled passenger and mail trains. Class 37s appeared on block steel trains to Workington, while Class 31s were increasingly common as replacements for the 25s and 40s. By the early 1990s, Class 60s were making regular forays along the coast on coal traffic.

Today, much of the railway infrastructure pictured on these pages is still extant. However the only regular freight flows along the coast today are irradiated nuclear fuel to Sellafield and calcium carbonate to Workington Docks. Classic traction on passenger trains made a brief comeback in 2015-18 when Direct Rail Services covered for a shortage of units, but those days are now consigned to history.

No. 40007 crosses the River Caldew on the Carlisle avoiding line with a trip working from Sellafield to Carlisle Yard on 24 August 1981. The train is conveying nuclear flasks loaded on first-generation Flatrol wagons, which BR had introduced around 1960. The bridge pictured here was damaged beyond economic repair by a derailed train in May 1984. Once it became clear that freight traffic could comfortably share the passenger tracks through Carlisle Station, the avoiding line was officially closed in the following year. No. 40007 was withdrawn from Healey Mills Depot in February 1983 and scrapped in January 1984.

Dalston Goods Yard closed as a public freight terminal in 1968, but the sidings lived on as an oil distribution terminal, serving customers in Cumbria and the Scottish Borders. No. 47190 sets back into the discharge siding with three two-axle tanks and nine bogie tanks on 23 July 1985. The working was the 03.30 departure from Grangemouth Refinery. Remarkably, Dalston Oil Terminal is still open today, long after the closure of most other rail-served oil terminals in Britain. Because of the short siding length today's trains are normally worked in three portions between Carlisle Yard and Dalston.

Nos. 37079 and 37042 accelerate away from Maryport with the 09.30 Workington-Lackenby empty steel carriers on 13 July 1983. The inward train had run overnight with steel bloom from Lackenby to Workington rail mill, a regular flow which had begun two years earlier after the closure of Workington's own blast furnaces. Maryport Station was unusual in having only one passenger platform, located on the northbound line. This meant that southbound passenger trains had to cross over before and after their station call, a situation which persists today. No.37079 was taken out of use in 1998 and earmarked for preservation before heading instead for the scrapyard in 2008. No. 37042 was more fortunate and is awaiting restoration on the Eden Valley Railway at the time of writing.

Sometimes referred to as 'Lakeland Colliery', the National Coal Board terminal at Maryport was a loading point for opencast coal delivered by road from various sites in West Cumbria. The rapid loading facility was brought into use in January 1980 and its rail infrastructure comprised a loading siding with weighbridge, a run round siding and a short siding for crippled wagons. Two connections with the main line enabled trains to arrive and depart in either direction. No. 40129 has just arrived at Maryport with the 06.55 empties from Workington on 13 July 1983. After loading, the train will head back to Workington Yard and then form a late morning departure to Fiddlers Ferry.

Located just over a mile north of Workington, Siddick Junction marked the divergence of the Cleator and Workington Junction Railway (CWJ) from the main coastal railway route. The CWJ had once served a number of iron and coal mines, but all that remained by the early 1980s was occasional military traffic to and from the Royal Naval Armaments Depot at Broughton Moor, reached via a reversal at Calva Junction. Siddick Junction Signal Box was normally switched out of use and was in a sorry state when photographed on 29 July 1985, as Class 108 cars 53963 and 54240 passed by with the 17.17 from Carlisle to Whitehaven. The box was replaced by a ground frame in 1988, which became redundant when the military traffic ceased in the early 1990s.

With a glimpse of Workington's industry visible on the skyline, No. 47347 heads north at Siddick Junction with the 06.42 Walton Old Junction (Warrington)-Carlisle freight working on 29 July 1985. This train called at several terminals as it made its way around the Cumbrian Coast, detaching and attaching traffic as required. On this occasion it has collected eleven wagonloads of rail from Workington, which will be distributed from Carlisle to their final destination.

Facing page: Workington Docks developed rapidly in the 19th and 20th centuries in line with the growth of the local iron and steel industry. The docks were also a convenient transhipment point for Cumbrian coal destined for Ireland, which in later years used merry-go-round equipment - enabling wagons to be discharged as they moved along at a constant slow speed - similar to that found at British power stations. No. 47372 is pictured edging forward with coal from Maryport on the morning of 30 July 1985. After the coal traffic ceased the sidings remained in use for other traffic including purified terephthalic acid, timber and calcium carbonate. Today, the only regular rail freight flow into Workington Docks is calcium carbonate from Aberdeen, hauled by Colas Rail.

One of the early Class 40s with disc headcodes instead of four-character headcode panels, No. 40082 skirts the passenger station at Workington on the goods lines with empty merry-go-round hopper wagons on 13 July 1983. This was the second train of the day to the loading point at Maryport. No. 40082 was allocated to the Liverpool Division of the London Midland Region at that time; it would be withdrawn from service in November 1984 and later scrapped.

This view from the south end of Workington Yard on 13 July 1983 gives a flavour of the industrial landscape that once stretched over several miles of the Cumbrian coastline. On the left, the former iron ore stocking area has become a massive scrapyard, with a few sidings next to the main line remaining in use for wagon storage and movements to and from the rail mill. Further sidings on the right contain an assortment of wagons including two rakes of elderly Covhop vehicles, still in use for powdered chemicals at that time. Heading south on the main line is No. 40129 with the 08.33 Maryport-Fiddlers Ferry coal train.

Rounding the curve just south of Harrington Station is No. 47245 *Linnet* with the 16.40 departure from Workington on 24 July 1990. This was a Speedlink wagonload service to Willesden Yard in North London. On this occasion the train is only carrying products from Workington rail mill, but it would make further scheduled calls at Corkickle and Warrington Arpley to attach and detach traffic as required. A distinctive feature of Harrington is the former late 19th century Methodist Church, converted into flats in the 1980s.

Facing page: After taking over from a Class 40 at Workington, No. 47292 heads south at Parton with the 08.33 Maryport-Fiddlers Ferry coal train on 13 July 1983. The derelict chimneys are a reminder of Parton's industrial past, when the village and its hinterland boasted collieries, an iron foundry, a tannery and a glassworks. Lumps of sea-polished glass can still be found on Parton Beach today. The exposed nature of the railway through Parton makes it vulnerable to storm damage and a ¾-mile stretch just north of Parton was reduced to single track to make room for stronger sea defences.

The daily Travelling Post Office (TPO) train was an unusual feature of Cumbrian Coast operations. The train ran from Workington to Whitehaven for parcels and then continued from Whitehaven to Huddersfield as a TPO service, calling at several intermediate stations on the Cumbrian Coast as well as Preston and Manchester Victoria. No. 47466 approaches Parton Station with the Workington-Whitehaven leg on 30 July 1985. A balancing northbound working ran in the early hours of the morning. Parton Signal Box was a London & North Western Railway (LNWR) structure which had 28 levers at the time of its closure in May 2010. The area is now controlled from Bransty Box at Whitehaven.

The original four-platform Whitehaven Bransty Station, opened in 1874, was reduced in BR days to three platforms – two on the through line towards Barrow-in-Furness and one north-facing bay. The LNWR station buildings were demolished in the early 1980s and replaced by a single-storey ticket hall. The suffix Bransty was dropped from the public timetable in 1968 but remained in use locally, as seen in this view dated 31 July 1985. Awaiting departure from the bay platform are Class 108 cars 54262 and 53955 on the 08.55 service to Carlisle. Just visible on the far right is the track that gave access to the harbour and Haig Colliery.

The north end of Whitehaven Station still had a fairly complex track layout when Class 108 cars M54235 and M53951 were photographed arriving with the 07.35 from Carlisle on 31 July 1985. The two tracks on the right converged at the south end of the station to enter the single-track Whitehaven Tunnel, which in historical terms was the final link in the string of railways forming the Cumbrian Coast Line. The 60-lever Bransty Signal Box was built in 1899 and still controls the station area today, albeit with many white levers following track rationalisation.

Facing page: In BR days Corkickle Sidings, located south of Whitehaven Tunnel, became the main freight yard for the Whitehaven area. Coal trains from Haig Colliery were tripped to Corkickle ready for their trunk haul south, and the yard also gave access to Preston Street Freight Depot and the Marchon Chemical Works – the latter reached by a rope-worked incline. With the late 1950s Corkickle No. 1 Signal Box visible on the right, No. 47226 waits to leave the yard with the 16.58 Workington-Dover Speedlink train on 30 July 1985. On this occasion the load comprises six sodium tripolyphosphate tanks from Corkickle to West Thurrock. The yard and its two signal boxes – Nos. 1 and 2 – closed in 1997, leaving a single track section from Whitehaven to St Bees.

Another view of the afternoon Speedlink departure from Corkickle, dated 24 July 1990, shows No. 47245 hauling a rather more varied load. The train is the same working as that pictured on page 13, but the two rail-carrying wagons in that photograph have been joined by six tanks of sodium tripolyphosphate for West Thurrock and ten discharged caustic soda tanks for Runcorn. They had all originated at Preston Street, which was the terminal for Marchon traffic after the rope-worked incline closed in 1986. The caustic soda tanks would be detached at Warrington.

Class 31 locomotives became established on nuclear flask workings in the late 1980s as BR began allocating traction to business sectors rather than geographical areas. Having said that, No. 31302 is carrying Trainload Petroleum livery rather than the Trainload Coal style that was the norm on nuclear traffic. The date is 2 July 1994 and the train is the 07.45 departure from Carlisle to Sellafield, pictured heading south from St Bees. The reason for the brake van in the middle is that the train comprises two portions, which have been combined at Carlisle for the final stage of their journey.

After tripping coal traffic between Maryport and Workington on the morning of 13 July 1983, No. 40129 headed south later in the day with this trainload of 29 UKF-liveried tank wagons from Corkickle, loaded with phosphoric acid for the fertiliser plant at Ince & Elton in Cheshire. The train has just passed the unstaffed platform of Nethertown Station. At that time BR also carried a weekly trainload of phosphoric acid from Corkickle to Barton-on-Humber, near Immingham, although it used its own wagon fleet for that traffic. The house perched between the railway and sea looks beyond repair but in fact it was restored in the late 1980s and is still habitable today.

Beach huts and the cooling towers of Calder Hall nuclear power station – part of the Sellafield complex – provide a contrasting backdrop in this scene dated 24 July 1990, as the 17.50 Barrow-in-Furness-Newcastle DMU heads north between Braystones and Nethertown. The first of the two Class 108 units comprises cars 54247 and 53964, which had been repainted in retro BR green livery in 1986. At the time of this photograph the unit was allocated to Heaton Depot near Newcastle, but was a regular performer on the Cumbrian Coast Line. It would be withdrawn from service in July 1992.

Facing page: No. 25201 makes its scheduled call at Sellafield Station with the 06.42 Warrington-Carlisle wagonload service on 30 July 1985. On this occasion it comprises four empty steel wagons returning to British Steel Workington. The train is framed by three artefacts from the steam age, of which the most unusual is the water crane. The 49-lever signal box was opened in 1918 and is still in use today, controlling the single-track section to St Bees as well as access to the nuclear reprocessing plant. The track layout at Sellafield Station is atypical, with an island platform between the up and down running lines and a further platform on the east side of the up line.

Sellafield nuclear reprocessing plant used to receive chemicals by rail alongside its staple traffic of irradiated fuel rods. Sentinel 0-6-0 diesel-hydraulic shunter No. 5, rebuilt by Thomas Hill in 1987, shunts tank wagons at the site on 1 April 1996. The middle track holds ICI caustic soda tanks which had come from Eastham in Cheshire, while the other two tracks are occupied by UKF nitric acid tanks from Ince & Elton. The caustic soda was later sourced from Runcorn and the nitric acid from Sandbach, hauled in both cases by Direct Rail Services, but in the end both these flows switched to road transport.

During the brief period when BR's trainload freight operations were divided between Transrail, Loadhaul and Mainline Freight, the remaining flows of chemicals on the Cumbrian Coast were operated by Transrail, who introduced a combined service for discharged nitric acid tanks from Sellafield and sodium tripolyphosphate from Corkickle to West Thurrock. These two flows make up the 09.10 Corkickle-Willesden train as it approaches Seascale on 2 July 1994. The locomotives are No. 31312 in BR Trainload Coal livery and No. 31229 in BR departmental livery; both are sporting the Crewe Cat Depot emblem. Unfortunately the sodium tripolyphosphate traffic would soon be lost to road and the train discontinued.

After the previous train has cleared the section to Bootle, the crossing gates at Drigg are opened for No. 47368 to continue its journey south along the Cumbrian Coast on 12 July 1983. The train is the 18.12 from Corkickle to Fiddlers Ferry, conveying coal from Haig Colliery at Whitehaven. The tall semaphore was replaced by a colour light signal shortly after the date of this photograph, but the manual crossing gates were still in use 40 years later. The station became unstaffed in 1967 but the attractive Furness Railway building on the up platform survived and later housed a tearoom and craft centre.

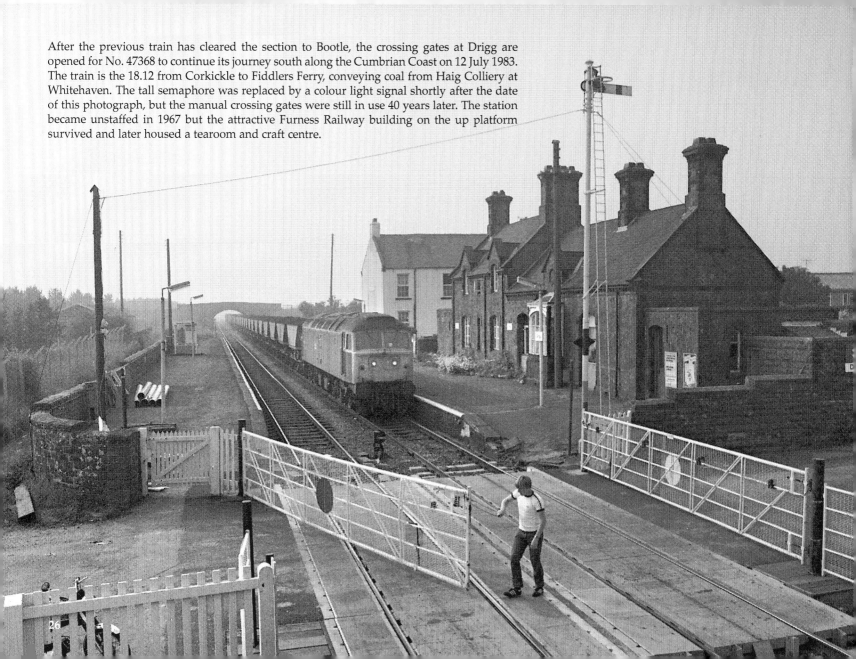

A siding was installed just north of Drigg Station in 1983 to serve the Low Level Waste Repository of the United Kingdom Energy Authority. The site itself had been in operation since 1959, taking low-level radioactive waste from nuclear power stations, hospitals and various other origins, all destined for long-term storage in covered vaults. Trains ran as required from Sellafield to Drigg, conveying waste initially in skips and later in steel containers. No. 25285 emerges from the Drigg Siding with empty skips for Sellafield on 31 July 1985. In recent years the siding has also received occasional trainloads of stone for capping the vaults.

Facing page: Heading north through Drigg on Saturday 27 February 1993 are Nos. 31302 and 31130 with the previous day's 16.32 Valley (Anglesey)-Sellafield flask train. The second locomotive is appropriately named *Calder Hall Power Station*. The load comprises nine flasks with an assortment of barrier wagons – including two former coal hoppers – and two brake vans, one in the middle and one at the rear. The first portion of the train had originated at Trawsfynydd and had been attached at Llandudno Junction. Standing prominently on the left is the Victoria Hotel, which opened not long after the arrival of the railway.

Classic traction made a welcome reappearance on Cumbrian Coast passenger services in 2015, thanks to a contract which Direct Rail Services won with Northern to provide cover for non-available diesel units. Two rakes of Mark II stock were initially topped and tailed by Class 37s, later switching to a single Class 37 at one end and a driving trailer at the other end. The last regular working took place in December 2018. Pushing its train away from Drigg on 16 October 2017 is No. 37401 *Mary Queen of Scots* with the 14.35 from Carlisle to Barrow-in-Furness. On the left the former goods shed still stands more than half a century after its railway use ceased, while on the right Drigg Signal Box – dating back to 1871 which makes it one of the oldest in the country – still fulfils its original role.

Two ICI caustic soda tanks provide the only traffic for the 16.58 Workington-Dover Speedlink train as it crosses the River Mite Estuary just north of Ravenglass on 31 July 1985. The traction is No. 47150, then allocated to Crewe Diesel Depot. An unnamed Class 47 in rail blue livery was about as ordinary as traction could get at that time but, like many of its classmates, No. 47150 had a varied career. Originally built as No. D1743 in 1964, it was based at depots on the Western, London Midland, Eastern and Scottish regions at various times. It then became a member of the Freightliner fleet upon privatisation and was withdrawn in 2008.

The two Royal Mail TPO vehicles stand out thanks to their recessed sliding doors and tiny windows as No. 47525 approaches Eskmeals with the Workington-Preston-Huddersfield mail train on 13 July 1983. This unlikely outlier of the TPO network lasted until September 1991, perhaps reflecting the remoteness of West Cumbria and therefore the usefulness of being able to sort mail on the move. The last TPO movements in the country took place in January 2004. The water belongs to the estuary of the River Esk, which rises in the Scafell range some 15 miles to the east. The hill protruding above the first TPO carriage is Muncaster Fell, a modest 758 feet above sea level.

Several Cumbrian Coast stations have retained their signal boxes because of level crossings, which would be costly and in some cases difficult to control remotely. Bootle is a case in point, where the 1871 Furness Railway box remains in use today. No. 25089 enters the station with the 17.22 Sellafield-Bridgwater flask train on 12 July 1983. In this instance the barrier wagons are former BR ferry vans, which had enjoyed only a short career carrying loads in their own right. Although the train's destination was Bridgwater, it could convey traffic for any of the nuclear power stations in Southern England, with portions being detached as required at Crewe.

Derby-built Class 108 DMUs took over Cumbrian Coast passenger services in 1969 and remained in charge until the arrival of Sprinter units in 1991. The drop-down windows of the 108s were fitted with bars because of the restricted clearances in Whitehaven Tunnel. Cars M53968 and M54251 depart from Silecroft – another location where a level crossing ensured the survival of the signal box – with the 13.50 from Whitehaven to Barrow-in-Furness on 12 July 1983. In the background are the slopes of Black Combe, the most south-westerly of the Lake District fells with its summit located just three miles from the coast.

A six-car Class 108 formation led by car M54263 is about to pass the 1891-built signal box at Millom with the 06.30 Carlisle-Preston service on 1 August 1985. This train took 3 hours 50 minutes to complete its coastal journey from Carlisle to Carnforth, with 33 intermediate calls including request stops. At that time there were half a dozen through workings around the coast in each direction, catering mainly for local journeys to and from the major towns. BR also provided short workings on the busier stretches, including Millom to Barrow-in-Furness.

A locomotive with electric train heating supply that was normally seen on passenger or parcels workings, No. 47539 *Rochdale Pioneers* passes Millom with a short rake of empty steel carriers on 31 July 1985. The train is the 06.42 Speedlink wagonload service from Warrington to Carlisle via Workington. The track on the right formerly led to Hodbarrow iron ore mines, which were once the largest facility of their kind in the world and operated until 1968. Today it is hard to believe that Millom was once a thriving industrial centre.

No. 25209 approaches Foxfield on 31 July 1985 with a special working from Kilmarnock to Derby, conveying the first Class 143 Pacer unit No. 143001 for testing. The train was running unfitted, i.e. without an automatic brake controlled from the locomotive, which meant that it was barred from the more direct West Coast Main Line and had to go via the Cumbrian Coast instead. The Class 143s themselves never had duties on the Cumbrian Coast, although they reached Carlisle while allocated to Heaton Depot on Tyneside. No.143001 later became No. 143601 and ended its main-line career in South Wales in May 2021; it has since been preserved.

Facing page: Unique on the Cumbrian Coast Line in having only an island platform, Foxfield Station is pictured on 31 July 1985, complete with its distinctive 1879-built signal box. No. 25173 passes by with a special working of empty mineral wagons from Tinsley to Workington, where they will be loaded with scrap metal. In busier times Foxfield Station was partly covered by a stone roof with a contiguous goods shed; it was also the junction for the Coniston Branch which closed to passengers in 1958 and goods in 1962. The station became an unstaffed halt in September 1967.

Facing page: The Furness Railway box at Askam, built in 1890 with a 22-lever frame, sets the scene for No. 25072 as it heads north with a special freight bound for Carlisle on 1 August 1985. Among the assortment of empty coal and ballast wagons is Class 08 shunter No. 08786 on its way to Carlisle after an overhaul. Until the 1980s it was common to move shunters around the network in freight trains; they could run at 45mph if their coupling rods were removed and their traction motors demeshed. No 08786 is still in existence today, having been sold to the Harry Needle Railroad Company for potential refurbishment and spot hire.

Barrow-in-Furness Station was destroyed during an air raid in May 1941 – the town was a prime target for the Luftwaffe because of its substantial steelworks and shipyard – and new station buildings were eventually completed by BR in 1957. In the early 1980s Barrow-in-Furness enjoyed several locomotive-hauled services to destinations such as Liverpool, Manchester and Crewe, using short rakes of Mark II stock. Pulling away on 14 July 1983 is No. 47441 with the 13.10 from Barrow-in-Furness to Liverpool Lime Street. The through sleeper train between Barrow-in-Furness and London Euston had recently been withdrawn at that time; it was later reinstated in the southbound direction only but ceased for good in 1990.

By the early 1980s little remained of the once extensive network of sidings in and around Barrow Docks. Apart from occasional nuclear flask movements to and from Ramsden Dock, the only regular customers were two domestic coal depots – Cart and Hackett – and a scrapyard located alongside Buccleuch Dock, reached via a spur from Salthouse Junction. At one time this spur had formed part of a through loop from Salthouse Junction to Ormsgill Junction, enabling freight trains to arrive and depart in either direction without passing through Barrow-in-Furness Station. No. 25221 shunts coal hopper and mineral wagons on the residual branch on 14 July 1983, before working back to Carnforth later in the afternoon. The coal traffic finished in 1984 when BR abandoned the use of traditional vacuum-braked wagons.

At Dalton Junction on the morning of 1 August 1985, the route has been set for the short cut to Park South Junction, a distance of just under one mile compared with 7½ miles via Barrow-in-Furness. No.31293 is in charge of the previous day's 22.15 Willesden-Workington Speedlink train, which on this occasion comprises a good mixture of wagons – nine empty sodium tripolyphosphate tanks, two empty steel carriers, one empty timber wagon and, just out of sight, six more empty steel carriers. At that time Class 31s were beginning to appear more frequently on the Cumbrian Coast Line, often on former Class 25 duties.

Making a change from the usual Class 47, Class 25 No. 25097 provides the haulage for the 10.16 Barrow-in-Furness-Nottingham train on 12 July 1983, pictured passing Dalton Station at speed. Visible just before the portal of Dalton Tunnel is the distant signal for Dalton Junction, where the Barrow loop diverges from the short cut to Park South Junction. The fine station building looked derelict at that time, having lost its resident staff in 1971; it has since been converted into a private house, with secure fencing separating it from the platform.

With its unusual platform layout recalling that of Sellafield, Ulverston Station is the setting for No. 25089 as it heads east with an engineers' spoil train on 12 July 1983. The reason for the platform arrangement here was to give 19th century passengers arriving from the Carnforth direction a step-free choice: They could either alight on the left and leave the station through the ticket hall or they could alight on the right for a cross-platform connection with the Lakeside Branch. Ulverston was something of a showpiece station for the Furness Railway, with its elaborate iron and glass canopies complementing an imposing station building and clock tower. Close examination of the platform benches reveals the Furness Railway's red squirrel motif. The station was Grade II listed in 1974 and has since been meticulously restored and repainted, making it a pleasure to visit today.

With the Sir John Barrow Monument standing prominently on Hoad Hill, commemorating a founding member of the Royal Geographical Society who was born in Ulverston, No. 47119 passes Plumpton Junction with a local trip working from Barrow-in-Furness to Carnforth on 1 August 1985. The track diverging to the left is the former Conishead Priory Branch, which remained in use to serve the Glaxo pharmaceuticals plant. Rail-borne deliveries to Glaxo ceased in 1994 and Plumpton Junction lost its purpose. The signal box closed in March 2000 and the railway was plain lined.

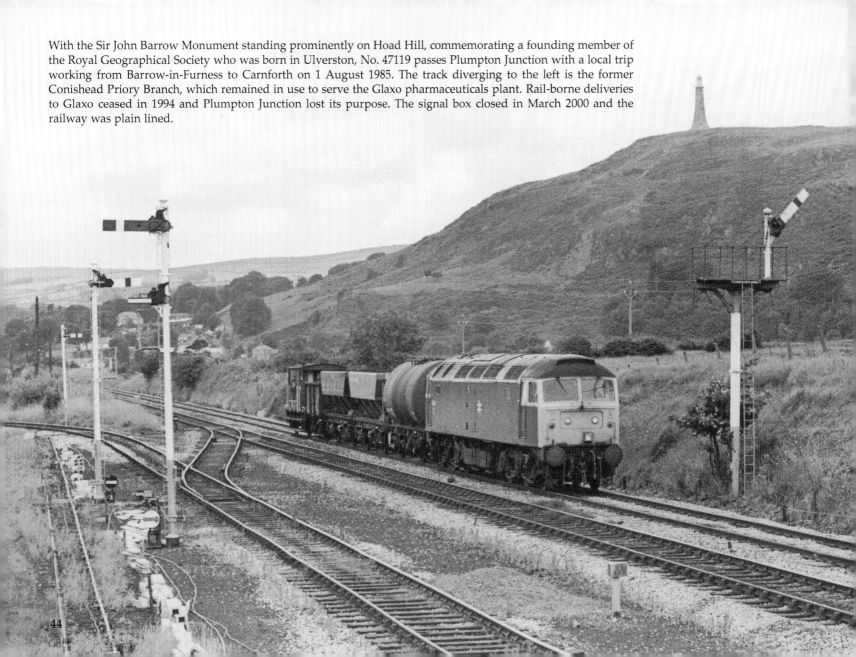

A visit to Grange-over-Sands on Saturday 16 May 1992 was rewarded by several locomotive-hauled trains, both freight and passenger. The 09.00 from Barrow-in-Furness to Manchester Victoria has just made its station call, with five BR Regional Railways Mark II coaches hauled by No. 47288 in Railfreight Distribution livery. This locomotive was withdrawn after sustaining serious damage from a derailment in September 1993. Like Ulverston, Grange-over-Sands Station is an architectural gem dating back to Furness Railway days. It was designed by the Lancaster architect Edward Graham Paley and completed in 1872. Today the station enjoys Grade II listed status and forms part of the town's conservation area. Substantial restoration was carried out in 1997/98 with support from the Railway Heritage Trust and various other bodies.

A pair of Class 108 units comprising cars M54239, M53958, 53976 and 54224 approaches Arnside Station with the 13.47 Whitehaven-Preston train on 1 August 1985. The signal box dates back to 1897 and is a well preserved example of Furness Railway architecture with its limestone walls, sandstone quoins and slate roof with terracotta ridge and finials; it gained a Grade II listing in 2013. The bracket signal behind the train once carried an arm for the branch to Hincaster Junction, which diverged to the right between the box and the platform. That branch closed to passengers in 1942 and to residual freight traffic from Sandside in 1971.

No. 31425 rattles over Arnside Viaduct on 23 July 1990 with the 17.53 Workington-Huddersfield mail and parcels train. The 51-span structure bridging the estuary of the River Kent was originally constructed for a single track in 1856 and was widened to two tracks in 1863. Its condition deteriorated in the 20th century, which led to a reduction in load capacity and the imposition of a 30mph speed limit. Network Rail commissioned the total replacement of the deck in 2010/11, giving a new lease of life to this important link from the West Coast Main Line to Ulverston and Barrow-in-Furness.

A 1970s Ford Escort waits for the passage of No. 40057 at the half-barrier crossing south of Silverdale Station on 14 July 1983. The train is the 16.58 from Corkickle to Northwich, conveying empty ICI tanks for reloading with sodium carbonate – also known as soda ash – at Lostock Works. The white-liveried wagons were a special design of 'Tip-Air' tank which could be tilted to ease the discharge of the lightweight cargo; a fleet of 60 of these wagons was introduced in 1975 and remained in use until 1986. No. 40057 suffered a bogie fracture and was withdrawn at Crewe Diesel Depot in July 1984. The half-barrier crossing at Silverdale was installed in June 1966 at a time when such installations were still something of a novelty; in recent times they have fallen out of favour because of the temptation for motorists to weave around the lowered barriers.